Preface to Grayscale

A new, relaxing, calm and surprisingly easy journey in coloring!
This book was created for those that love to color and the coloring enthusiast that says:
"I wish I knew how to create a beautiful work of art."

Coloring in the gray or Grayscale Coloring is all about adding color to the pictures using your medium of choice: colored pencils, markers, watercolor, acrylic paint or oil pastels
.

As You choose a color palette and the aspects of the picture that will benefit from working between the dimensions of black and white, your masterpiece is stylized with your personality and ready to hang for showcasing your finished work to friends, family and/or the world

Printed in the United States of America

First Printing, 2018

ISBN 9781797508061
Publisher

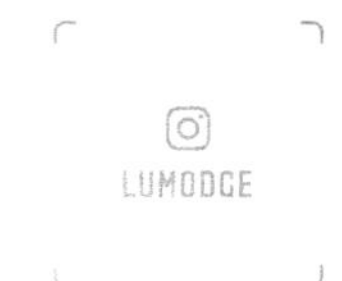

Instagram/Youtube : @lumodge
Email: lumodge@gmail.com

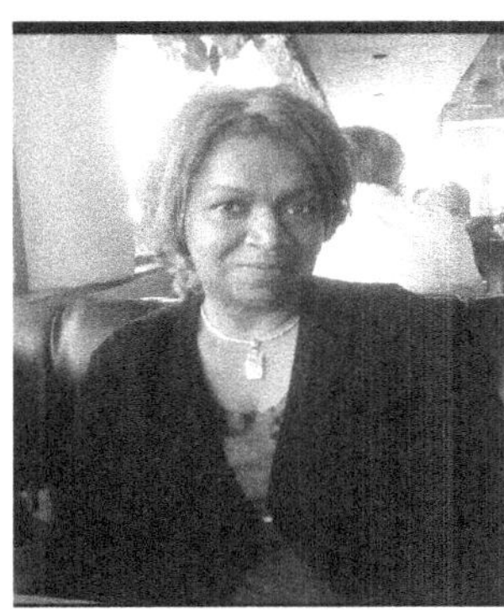

My recent thoughts have rendered me a life quote:
"Maturity, brings about great focus."

Another quote that has been occupying my mind these days is one by Norman Vincent Peale:
"Shoot for the moon. Even if you miss, you'll land amongst the stars."

As a mother of 3 adult children from Camarillo, California I have found that locating youors like; Author, Illustrator, Tutor, Artist, Photographer and Event Planner, has lead me on a path that is both imaginative and insightful. The objectives is the same: **To help others achieve their dreams and to leave our world in a better place.**

My desire is that wr joy in the midst of the journey is essential to being creative.

In this stage of my passion, bouncing between my many expressive endeavhatever creative endeavor you have located me through, may it leave a lasting and enjoyable imprint that will inspire you to find your own creative voice. **Selah**.

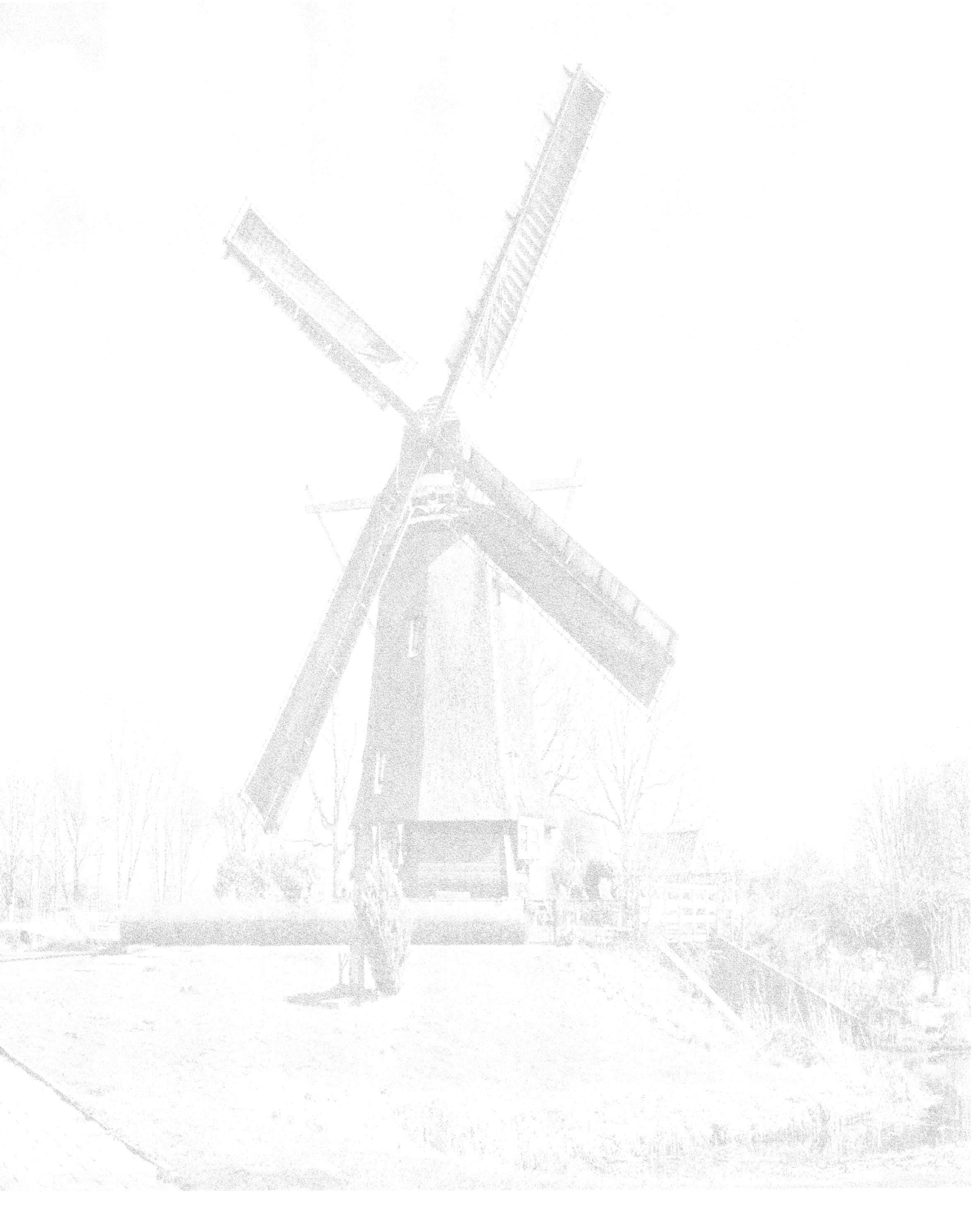

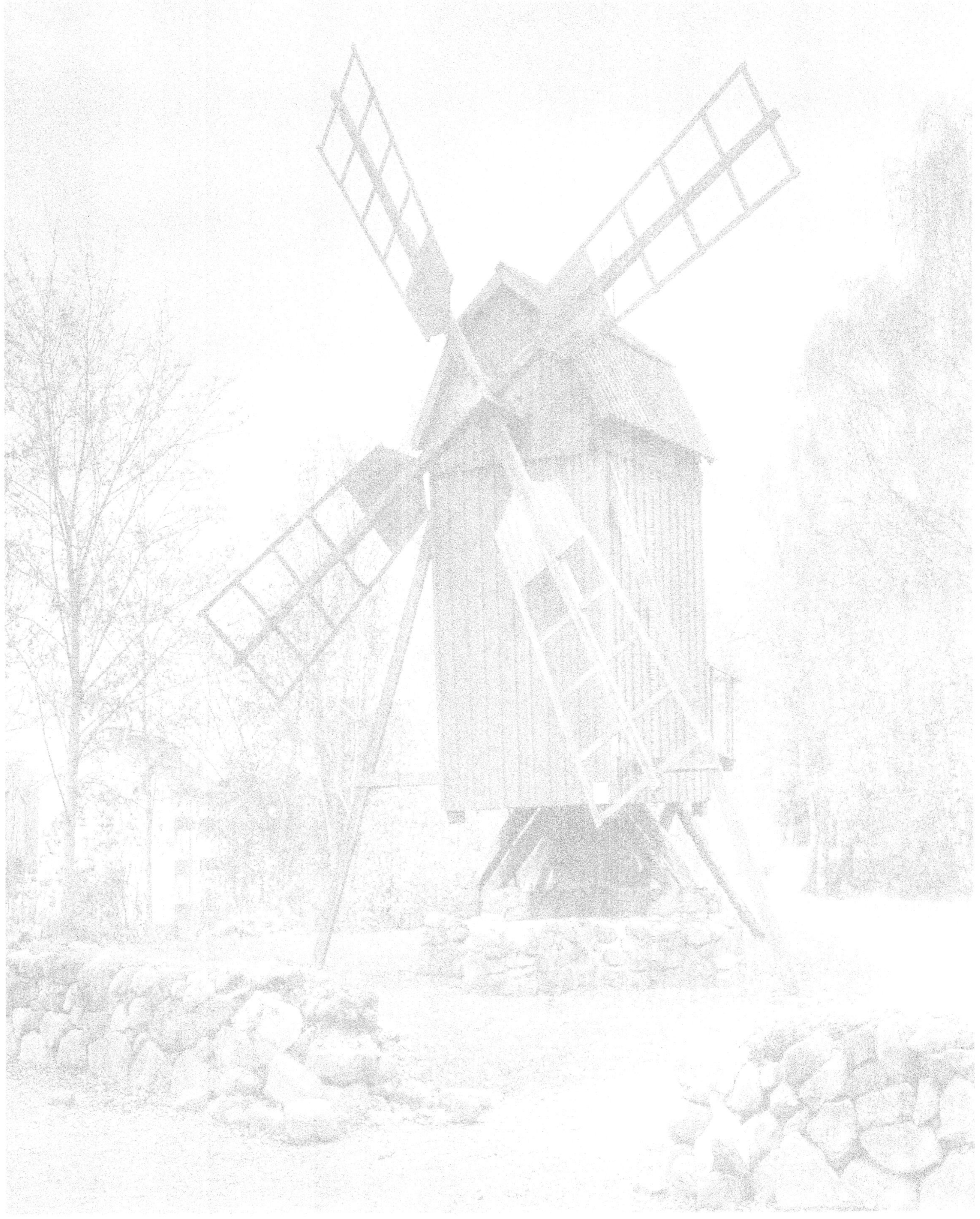

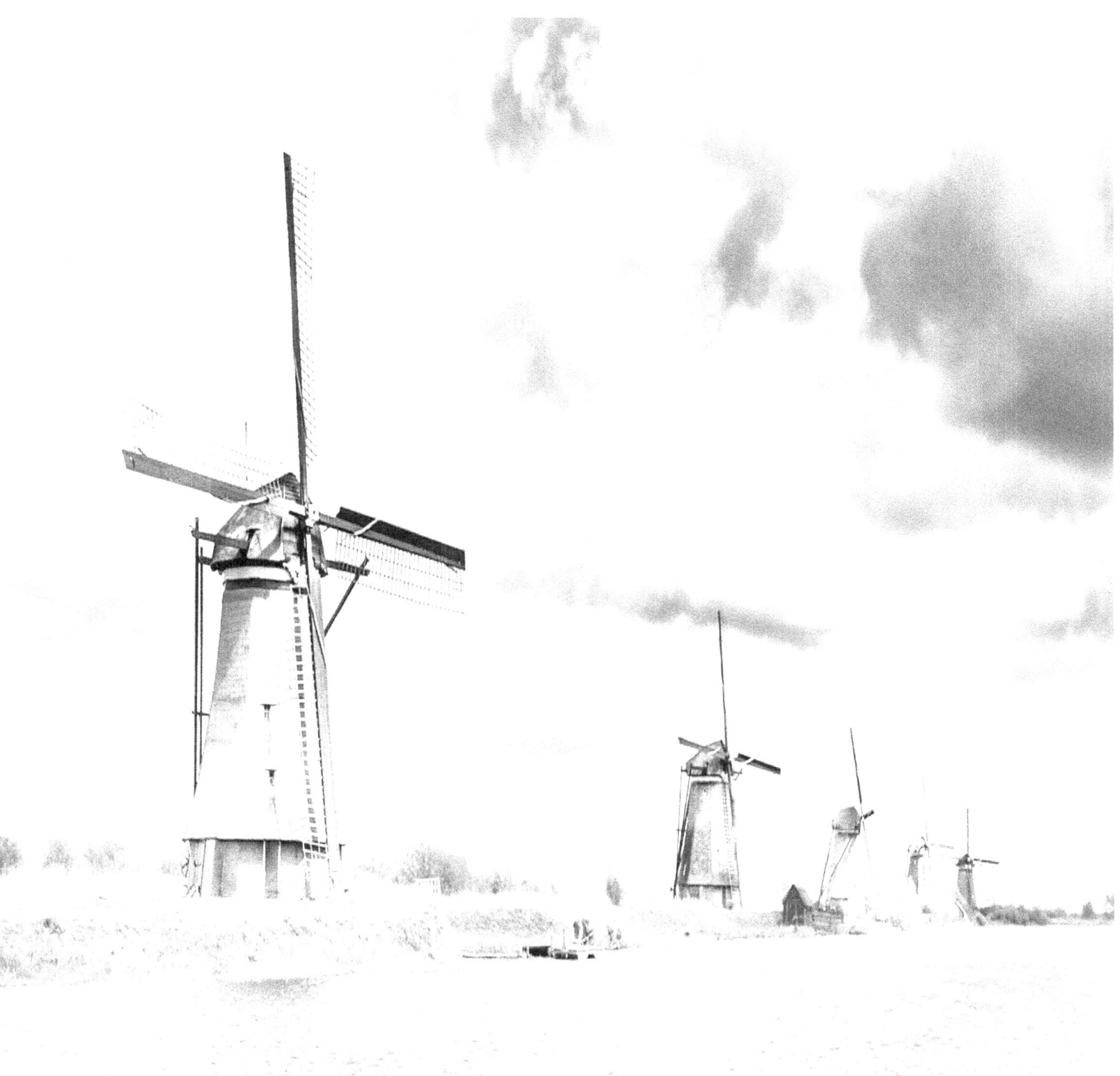

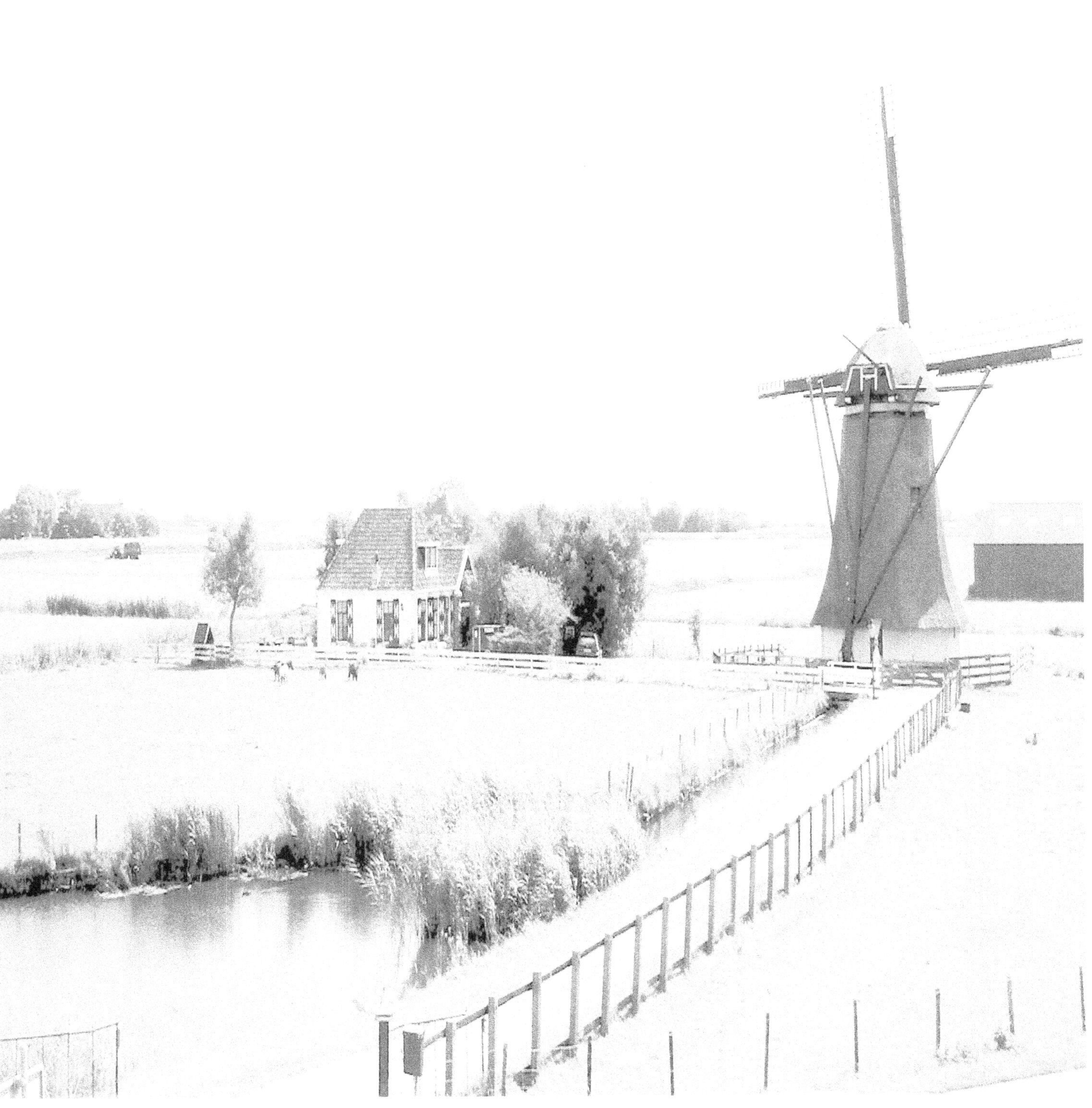

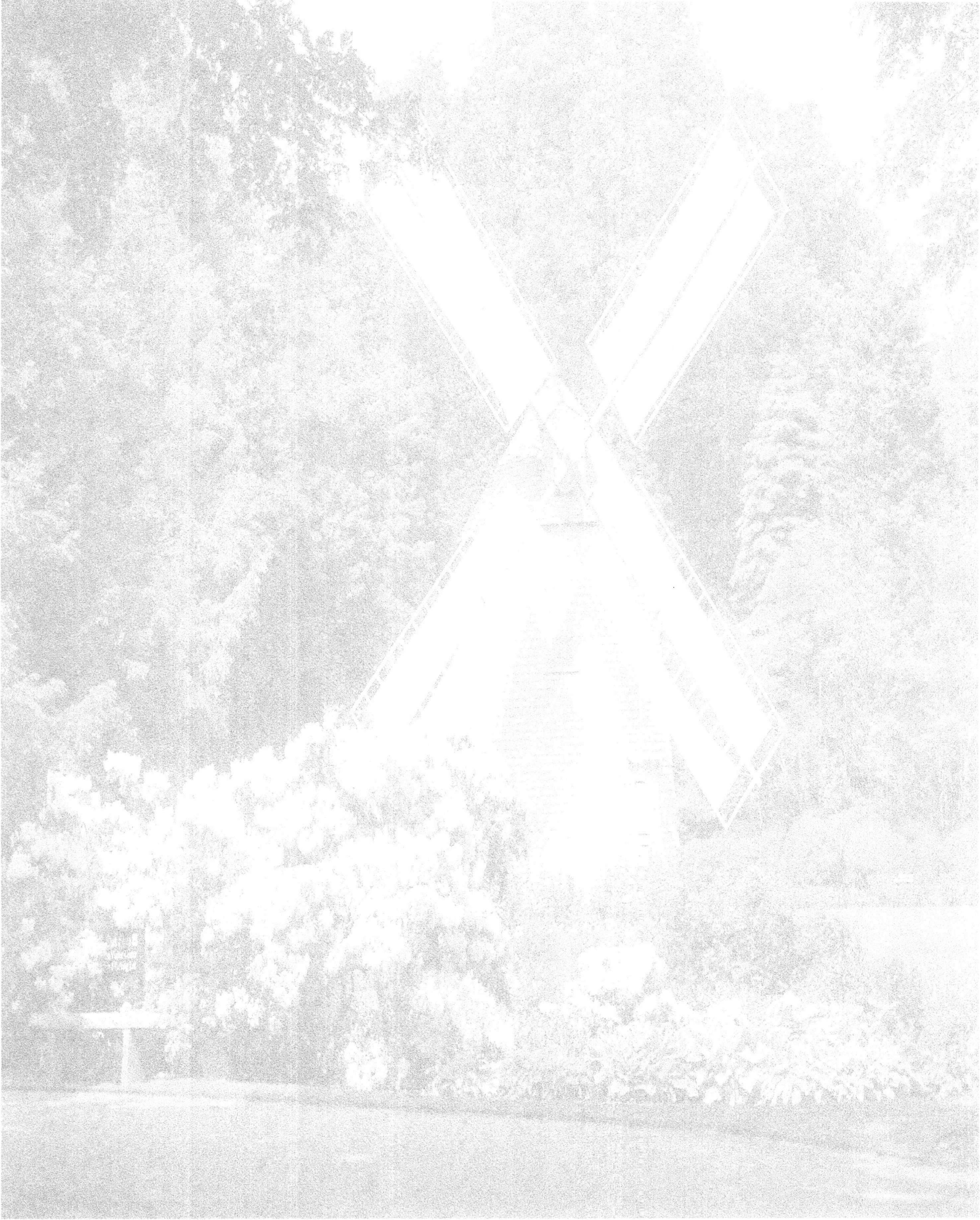

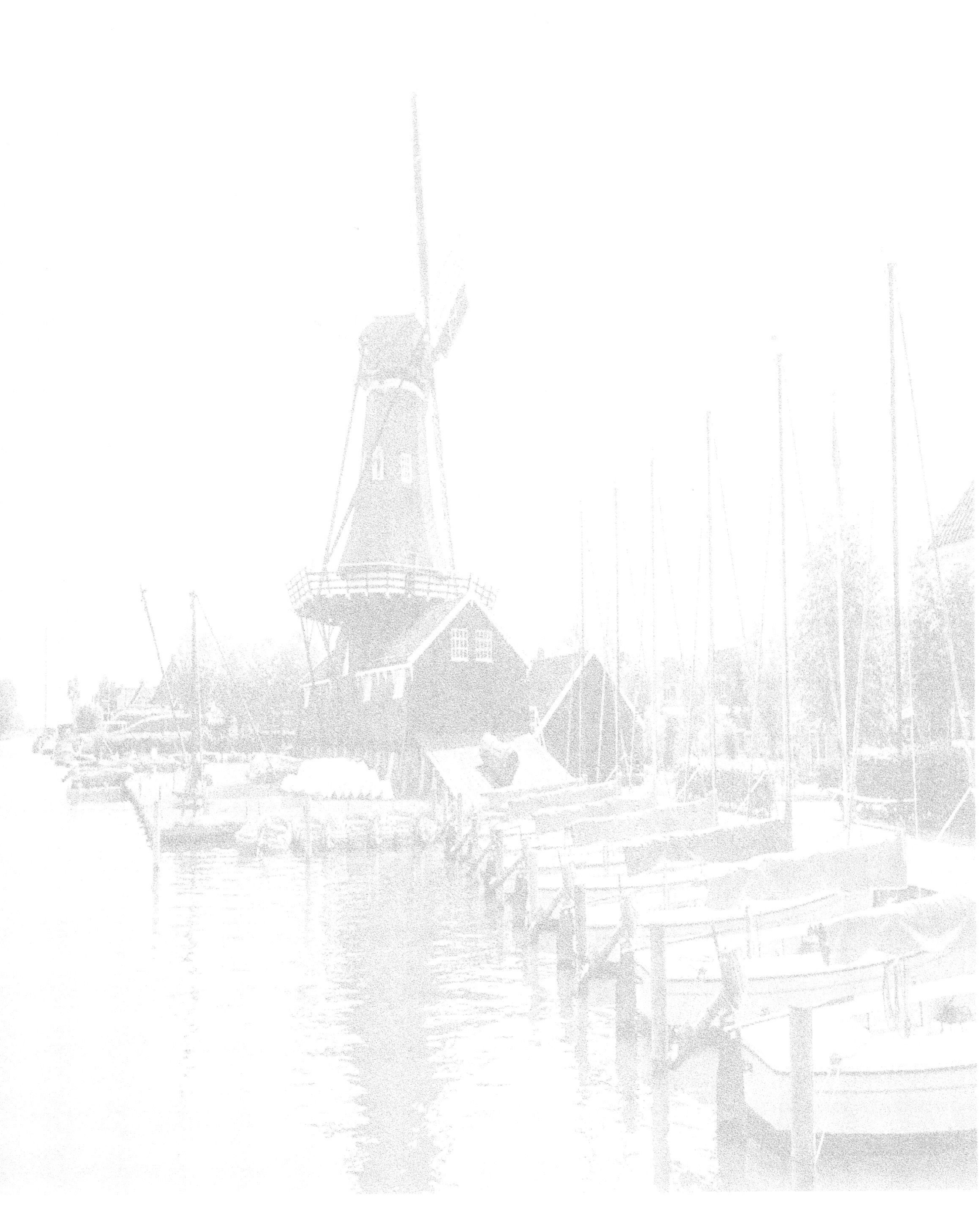

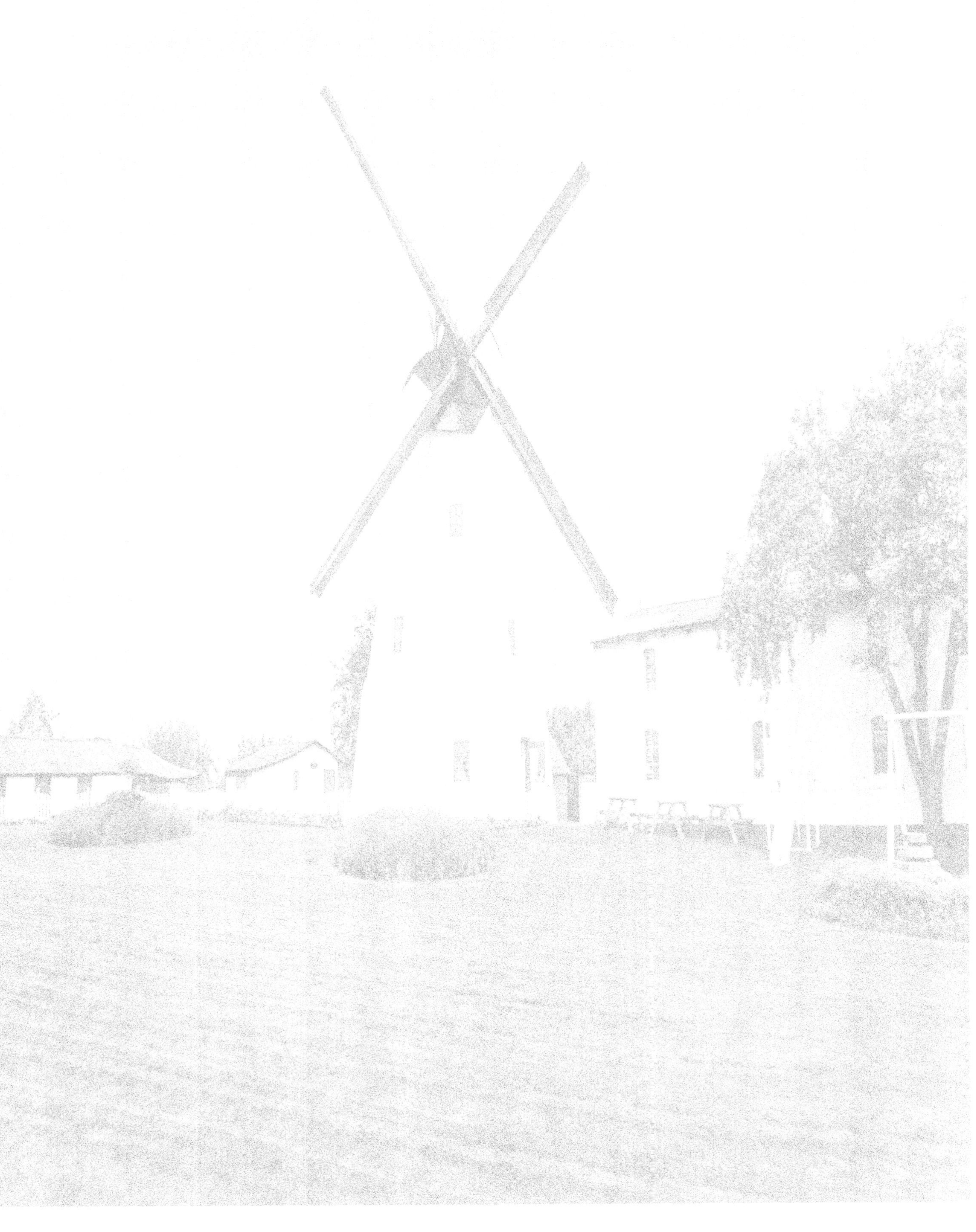

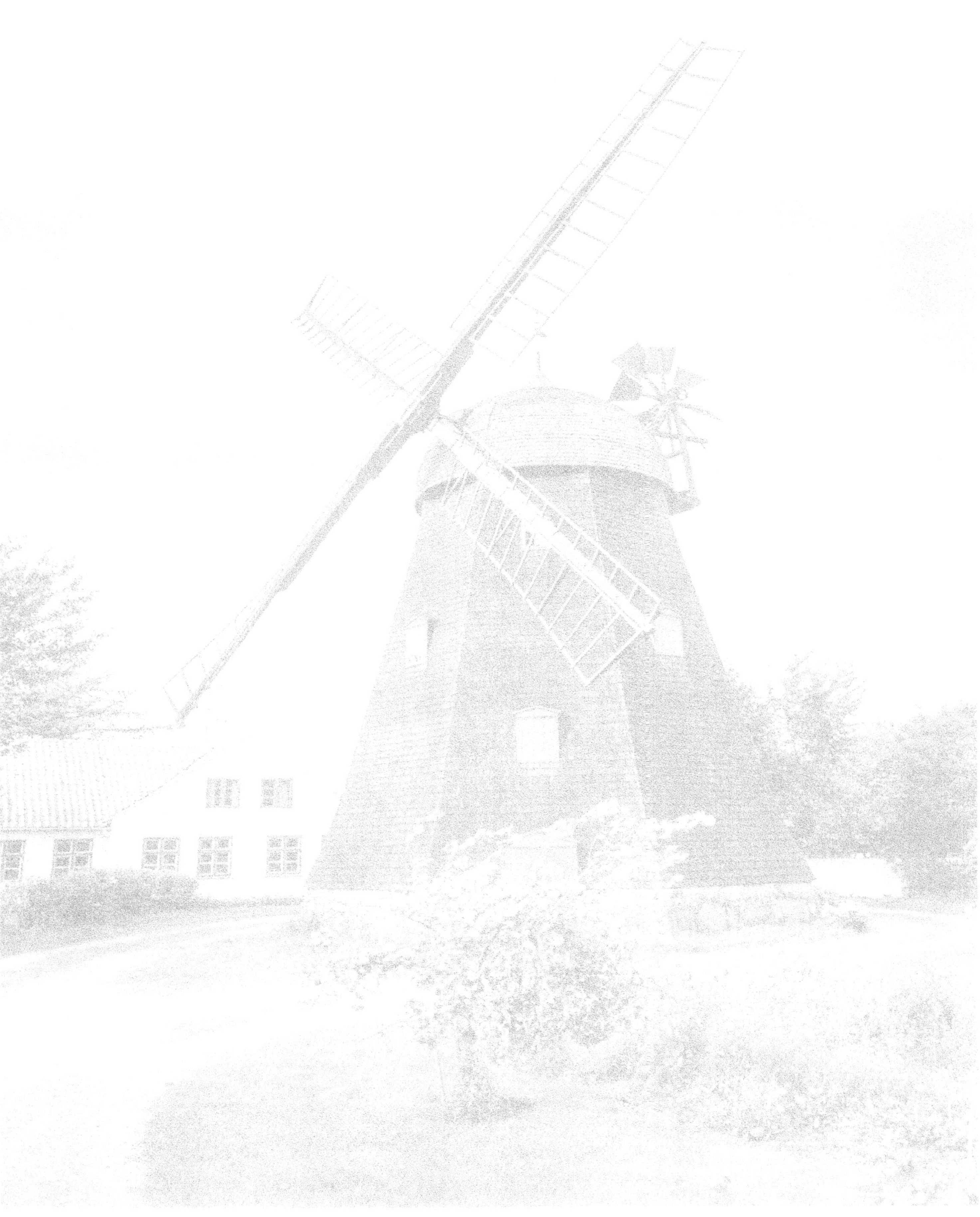

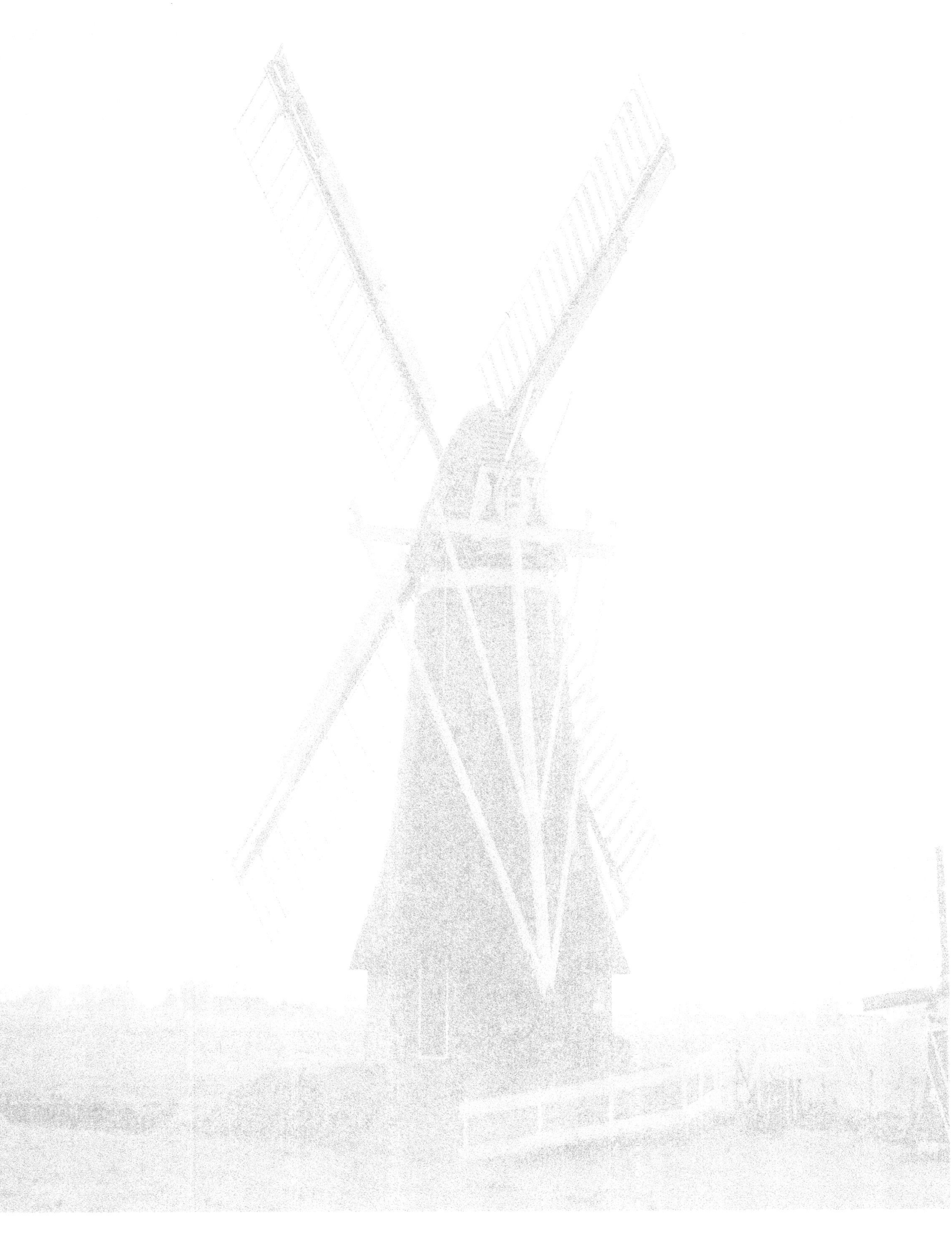

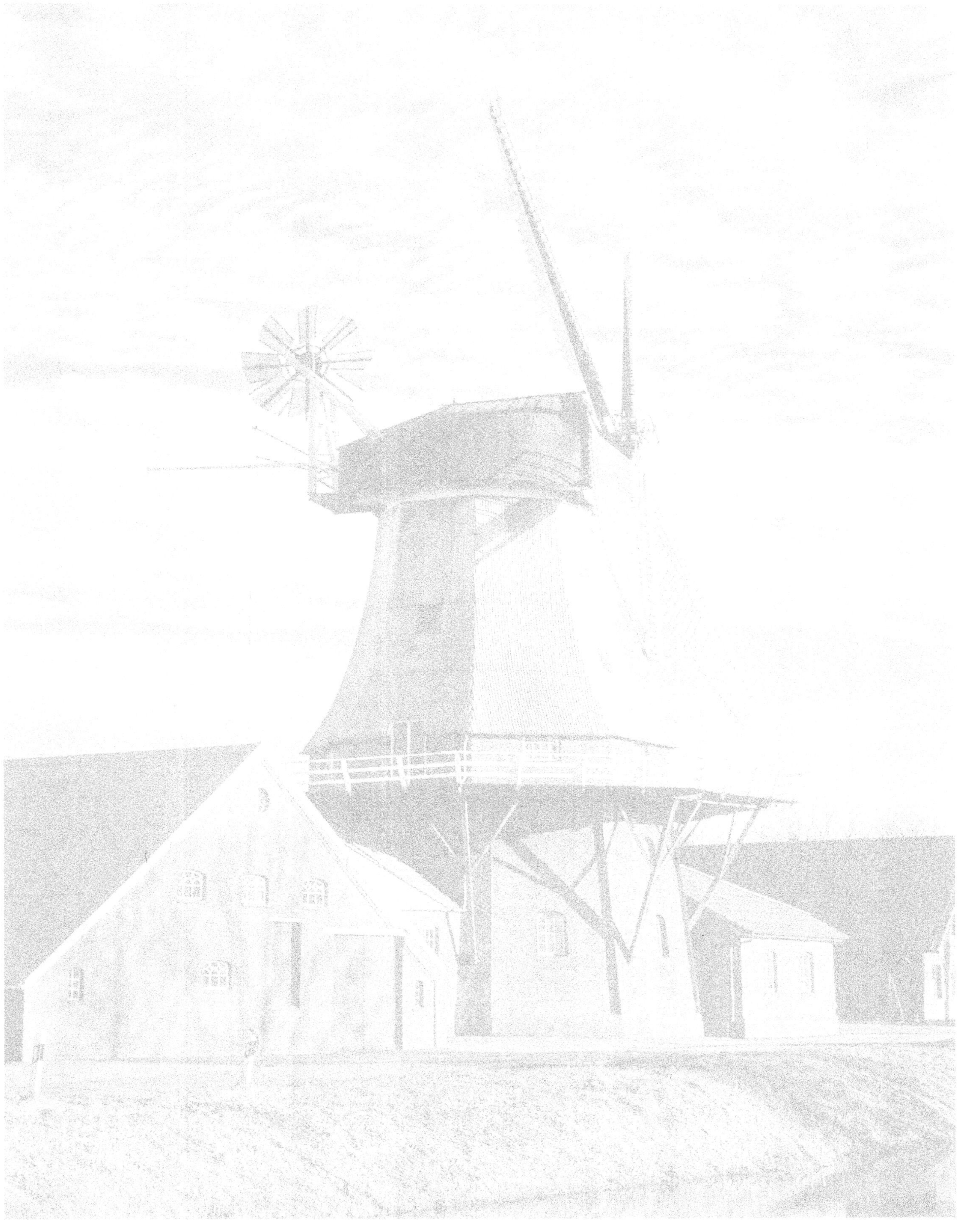